Who The Druids Were And Their Ancient Signs And Symbols Explain

Albert Churchward

Kessinger Publishing's Rare Reprints

Thousands of Scarce and Hard-to-Find Books on These and other Subjects!

- Americana
- Ancient Mysteries
- Animals
- Anthropology
- Architecture
- Arts
- Astrology
- Bibliographies
- Biographies & Memoirs
- Body, Mind & Spirit
- Business & Investing
- Children & Young Adult
- Collectibles
- Comparative Religions
- Crafts & Hobbies
- Earth Sciences
- Education
- Ephemera
- Fiction
- Folklore
- Geography
- Health & Diet
- History
- Hobbies & Leisure
- Humor
- Illustrated Books
- Language & Culture
- Law
- Life Sciences
- Literature
- Medicine & Pharmacy
- Metaphysical
- Music
- Mystery & Crime
- Mythology
- Natural History
- Outdoor & Nature
- Philosophy
- Poetry
- Political Science
- Science
- Psychiatry & Psychology
- Reference
- Religion & Spiritualism
- Rhetoric
- Sacred Books
- Science Fiction
- Science & Technology
- Self-Help
- Social Sciences
- Symbolism
- Theatre & Drama
- Theology
- Travel & Explorations
- War & Military
- Women
- Yoga
- *Plus Much More!*

**We kindly invite you to view our catalog list at:
http://www.kessinger.net**

THIS ARTICLE WAS EXTRACTED FROM THE BOOK:

Signs and Symbols of Primordial Man

BY THIS AUTHOR:

Albert Churchward

ISBN 1564591050

READ MORE ABOUT THE BOOK AT OUR WEB SITE:

http://www.kessinger.net

OR ORDER THE COMPLETE
BOOK FROM YOUR FAVORITE STORE

ISBN 1564591050

which shows the time that the Stellar doctrines were changed into Solar and the Eschatology.

Their kings, in numerous instances, worshipped in groves. Though the practice was afterwards discontinued, yet there is sufficient to show that the custom had formerly been prevalent. "The Lord God appeared to Abraham by the Oak of Moreh." The word אררה should be translated "oak" not "plain" as in our version, see Gen. xii. 6. "He pitched his tent by an oak tree." Jacob adored his God through the same medium, and buried his dead beneath an oak, and this mystic adoration of the oak survived after many centuries had elapsed. "Joshua took a stone and raised it up under an oak that was by the Sanctuary of the Lord" (Joshua xxiv. 26). *Pliny* mentions the high esteem which the Druids had for the oak.

In very early times the Deity was adored only in the open air: the worshippers' astronomical acquirements had taught them that certain stars rose when Spring, Summer, Autumn and Winter commenced, while their acquaintance with various astronomical occurrences led them to commemorate them by raising up stones, which were generally in a circular form. "And Moses rose up early in the morning and builded an altar under the hill and twelve pillars, according to the twelve tribes "— twelve signs of the Zodiac. The manner in which these stone temples were erected may be more fully gathered from other parts of the Pentateuch (Deut.). "So Joseph was buried in the temple of Gerizim." See also temple of Gilgal—Joshua iv. 5.

Stonehenge may be said to be analogous to one of these temples: its stones are arranged in the same manner as were those of the Israelites and its magnitude and rude grandeur proclaim that the people who raised the ponderous blocks of stone here, as well as in other parts of Britain, were both learned and powerful.

Joshua, the builder of the structure at Gilgal, assembled the Israelites in the new temple. He said, " When your children in future ages shall ask their fathers *what mean these stones?* ye shall tell them that these were erected as an acknowledgment to the Almighty God, that ye might fear the Lord your God for ever."

The seven stones set up at Stonehenge and elsewhere represent the seven giants who were petrified and changed into enormous stones. These also stood for the seven stations of the pole in the circuit of precession or the circle of Sidi. Under one title, Stonehenge was called the circle of Sidi or the circle of the seven. The Mexicans also have a class of gods who had been turned into stone. These powers could resume a movable shape when they pleased. Becoming petrified as stones would denote the condition in which they stood as fixed figures of the pole, and known to the astronomers that all in turn would resume a movable shape as gods of the pole stars. They constituted the typical foundation of the heptanomis that was built in the heavens and repeated by the mound builders in many lands on earth. This was part of the Stellar mythology brought on and merged into Solar.

In Ireland, as well as in England, a vast number of these monuments exist, but it is in the Scottish Islands that they are discovered in their finest preservation. In France, as well as in other parts of the Continent, they are also to be met with. A very little thought will show how well they were calculated to obtain the end desired. The feelings of the devotee on entering these mystic temples must have been indescribable; the solemnity of the surrounding scenery, the vast and silent concourse of attentive people, the rude, romantic, imposing magnificence of the structure, the Arch-Druidical prophet, emerging from beneath the mysterious trilithic altar and announcing to the wondering multitudes the answer he had heard in whispers from his God;—all this must have created a religious exaltation, intense and overwhelming.

It has been said that when the ancients experienced any signal favour or received any gift at the hands of their Deity, it was their usual custom to erect a stone in remembrance of the blessing. In the British Isles pillars of this description are very numerous, and this practice in our Isles was just as prevalent amongst the Israelites.

We wish to point out here that the religion as practised by the patriarchs differed somewhat from that which Moses afterwards taught. The old patriarchs worshipped God under the name of Baal, sacrificed in high places, adored in groves, planted oaks, intermarried with their immediate relatives, all of which was afterwards forbidden by Moses; in other words, it was a change from the Stellar and Lunar into Solar Mythos.

We mention this because some divines have stated that there was no connection at all between these religions, but that the Druids were infidels. They quote Scripture of much later date to try and prove their statements. They have, however, either ignored the first part of our volume of the sacred law or overlooked it in their anxiety to prove that these ancient people were idolaters. The above will prove the contrary.

Bel—when the Druids and others fell from their original purity of manners—became, as it did among the Israelites, a title with a different meaning, and the reason for the change was that at first it was the Stellar mythos of the Egyptians, and as the Egyptians changed this into Lunar and Solar, and finally formulated the Eschatology, so all those who had intercommunicated with them did the same, and everything was gradually brought up to date—no doubt it took many years to achieve. Bel or Set Anup or El Shaddai was the primary Pole Star God South until he was deposed by Horus I., God of the Pole Star North.

Their sacrifices were the same. The mensuration of time by night and day was the same. The Israelites kept their Sabbath from sundown (Levit. xxiii. 32). *Cæsar* says the Druids did the same. "*Galli se omnes, ab Dite patre prognatos predicunt, adque ab Druidibus proditum dicunt. Ob eam causeam, spatia omnis temporis non numero dierum, sed noctium finiunt, dies natales et mensium et annorum initia, sac observant at noctum dies subsequatur.*"

The manner of the burial of the dead was the same among the Druids, Israelites and Egyptians.

In fact, we find that the ancient Egyptians, Israelites and Druids all adored the same God and the rites of all were similar. The Egyptian PTAH—I am all that has been, is, or shall be—to whom they ascribed every attribute of nature, is the same God as the God of the Israelites and Druids, and all had the same religious ceremonies.

Brother Gould, in his "History of Freemasonry," vol. ii., says: "The connection of Druids with Freemasonry has, like many other learned hypotheses, both history and antiquity obstinately bent against it, but not more so, however, than its supporters are against history and antiquity, as from the researches of recent writers may be easily demonstrated."

It is obvious that *Brother Gould's* "researches" must be

altogether too recent for him to be able to discuss the question he here makes bold to dispute, for all facts show that some of the assertions contained in his work are " fables."

We have only brought forward facts to prove the connection of the ancient Egyptians and the Druids, which no one can dispute, because these facts exist.

Brother Gould also states that Julius Cæsar did not mention the British religion (Druids) at all. The above quotation from *Cæsar* has evidently not come within *Brother Gould's* "researches." He cannot have made any deep study of the antiquity of the subject, for the monuments that still exist and the decipherment of the hieroglyphics on the same distinctly prove that the views we have stated are correct : nevertheless, his recent history of the craft is certainly most elaborate and complete to date.

When the Romans, under Julius Cæsar, invaded Britain, the inhabitants were famous, even among foreign nations, for the superior knowledge of the principles and the great zeal for the rites of their religion. History informs us that the Druids, the Gymnosophists of India, the Maji of Persia and the Chaldeans of Assyria had all the same religious rites and ceremonies as practised by their Priests, " who were initiated " to their order, and that these were solemnly sworn to keep the doctrines a profound secret from the rest of mankind. They never committed anything to writing and were the same as the Priests of Egypt, from whom they obtained them, and their laws were the same as the so-called laws of Moses. The fact that the similitude or rather identity of their opinions, institutions and manners of these orders of ancient Priests, though they lived under different climates and at no great distance from each other, without intercourse, amounts to this :—that all these opinions, institutions and beliefs simply flowed from one source—Egypt. *Cæsar*, *Diodorus* and *Mela* all agree to this, and *Mela* tells us that they taught the doctrine of the immortality of the souls of men—it was the Eschatology of the Egyptians.

It is of no use to take into account what all of these " preached to the public." It is not possible to bring women and the common herd of mankind to religious piety and virtue by the pure and simple dictates of reason ; it is necessary here to call in the aid of superstition, which must be nourished by fables and portents of various kinds, and this we find the Druids did, and possessed unbounded power, before the advent of the Romans, over all and everything; but as the Romans gained control in this island, so the power of the Druids gradually declined, until it was quite destroyed as a civil factor. Those, however, who would not submit to the Romans, fled to Ireland, Scotland and the smaller isles, where they supported their authority for a long time after, up to the eleventh and twelfth centuries A.D. This we see from the following law made by Canute :—" We strictly discharge and forbid all our subjects to worship the God of the Gentiles." The Druids had one chief or Arch-Druid in every province, who acted as High Priest. These had absolute authority over all the others and he was elected from amongst the most eminent by a plurality of votes. *Cæsar* acquaints us that they taught their disciples many things about the nature and perfections of God, and that there was only one God, the Creator of heaven and earth. One name, under which they worshipped Him, was Esus or Hesus or Harits, which is their name for Horus. But their secret doctrines were never communicated to the bulk of mankind; these were carefully kept concealed. The consecrated groves, in which they performed their religious rites, were fenced around with stones, to prevent any person entering, except through the passages left open for that purpose, and these were guarded by some inferior Druids to prevent any stranger from intruding into their mysteries, in the same way that we find the ancient Egyptians all had their entrances guarded by the " Cutters " (Tylors). The Druids taught the wisdom of Egypt in the British Isles ages before the present volume of the Sacred Law was heard of. They had the Ark of Nu as the ark of the seven Kabiri and the seven Hohgates the seven who were companions of Arthur in the ark.

With the general consent of the whole there were three orders. The Arch-Druid, who was elected to that position by all the other Druids, it not being a hereditary office, fixed on the most beautiful oak-tree in the grove and then performed the rite of consecration. All the side branches having been first cut off, he proceeded to join two of them to the highest part of the trunk, so that they extended on either side like the arms of a man and formed in the whole the shape of a cross Swastika. Above the insertion of these branches and below they inscribed in the bark of the wood the word "Thau" and before it performed their most ancient rites. This sign is also found occupying the centre of the triangle

That this sign of the Swastika was found in Britain, 3000 B.C. until 300 A.D. will prove pretty conclusively that the time of the exodus of the "Druids" from Egypt was at the time they had the Swastika, after they had converted this from the figures of the four quarters and before they had changed the same into the Ankh Cross by evolution, probably more than twenty thousand years ago if *Flinders Petrie* is right in his dates as to his recent discoveries at Abydos. The meaning of each is the same. The conversion of this sign—"Swastika or Gammadion," another name of it, and there are a great many different names for the same sign in various parts of the world—into the Latin Cross was effected by the Christians in this way, as may be seen on a Runic stone from Sweden.

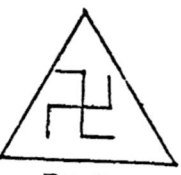

FIG. 83.

Thus we see how one form of the Cross, now used amongst the Christians, originated direct from the sacred symbol of the Swastika, without following the evolution of the Ankh Cross which some others have, in those countries where the practice of the Osirian doctrines had been in progress for thousands of years after the exodus of the Druids from Egypt, probably at the period when they had just evolved the Solar mythos from the Stellar and Lunar; and the above would lead us to believe that there was little intercommunication, eschatologically, or any interference with them until the time that the Romans brought the doctrine of Christianity amongst them, then converting their long-used ancient and sacred symbols into an "up-to-date" form of the time.

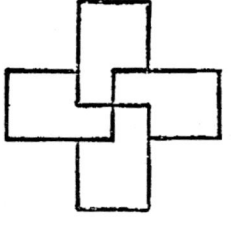

FIG. 84.

We think that this must be so, because of the very important figures of the earliest form of the Swastika, in the form of four Human Figures, which is still preserved and can be seen in Scotland as shown here (see chapter on "Cross"). And the god of the 4 quarters is depicted as Atum-Ra in the *Ritual* (chap. lxxxii.). The divine man described by Plato was bicussated and stamped

188 SIGNS AND SYMBOLS OF

upon the universe in the likeness of a Cross. The new heaven in the book of Revelation was formed according to the measure of a man (Rev. xxi. 17), which was the old Stellar heaven founded on the 4 cardinal points represented by the Swastika Cross of the 4 quarters, as seen here in Mexico and many other parts of the world.

Probably this is of much greater importance in deciphering the true meaning and origin than any other form we have met with. The Egyptian original of this will be shown later on, and there cannot be any question of identity between the two. If formed during the Stellar mythos it would mean or represent the four quarters. (*See* Appendix I.)

This is also represented by another sign—viz. two triangles—as follows, which has the same meaning and is well known to all R.A.M.'s, and has by some been named the Seal of Solomon (see origin of triangles). The origin of the double triangle was the double triangle in "Ares," therefore Celestial, as may be seen on any celestial globe. The Druids had the three feathers

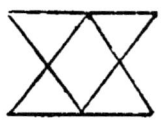

Fig. 85.

in use amongst them in the form of \|/ or \|/ called "three rods or rays of light," signifying the eyes of light or the radiating light of intelligence shed upon the Druidical circle It is also the name "I.A.U." I.A.U., the son of Ptah—*i.e.* Jesus, son of the Father, so the three rods stand for "The Light of the World," and the Druids used it as a sacred sign and symbol, the same as the Makalanga use and recognise it. The Makalanga, the children of the Sun, in South Africa, have this sign carved or tattooed on their bodies, and consider it a most sacred sign, and "the name of the great giver of light." They do not know the origin of this, but their ancestors handed it down to them, and so they still mark their bodies with this device and treasure the meaning and name in a most sacred and solemn way. Jesus tells his disciples, "Ye are the light of the world" (Matthew v. 14). He himself was called by Simon "a light to lighten the nations" (Luke ii. 32), and he assumed the name of "the light that is come into the world" (John iii. 19); and in another place he says, "I am the light of the world" (John viii. 12), and again, "yet a little while is the light with you" (xii. 35); "I am come a light into the world, whosoever believeth in me should not abide in darkness" (xii. 46). The Central Americans also had the three rays of light to represent the same, and four rays of light in this form to represent the four children of Horus.

The symbol was appropriated by King EDWARD III. and adopted as one of his badges. It was borne by his son, the Black Prince, and by other Princes of Wales, and still is as the three feathers, which was the original, and is seen as this.

These feathers are also a sign of ancient Egypt (Pierret 754). I.U. is older than I.A.U.; in fact, it is the oldest Egyptian name of Jesus. See later on how this has been altered. Two feathers first represented I.U. and then three as I.A.U.; also the two lives—spiritual and earthly: and it is a significant fact that I.U. or I.A.U., the son of PTAH, should have the original handed down and adopted here, as an earthly type of the son of the King.

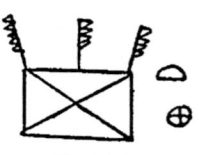

FIG. 86.

The fact that these rods are rods in one case and feathers in another, does not alter the meaning or change the original. The Broad Arrow occurs as a mark of the Royal Household in 1386. It also shows that the Druids, although practising and belonging to the doctrines of the Solar mythos, had brought on with them and used the symbols of the first or Stellar mythos. Another important sign, and the most sacred amongst them, was the first evolution of the Cross—viz. the Swastika, as we have shown.

These three rods or rays of light or symbol for I.U. are still worn and used by *our present Druids*, and anyone can see the symbol on the Caps worn by those of the highest degree; how many of them know its meaning? It has identically the same meaning as the supreme council wear on the Caps the triangle; how many of the S.C.'s know this or what its signification is? but the S.C. should have the triangle with the apex downwards to be correct, as the triangle as they wear it was originally the name for Sut or El

Shaddai or Bel; it was certainly appropriated by Horus later, but the triangle belonging to Horus only was ▽ apex downwards. (*See* Appendix 2.)

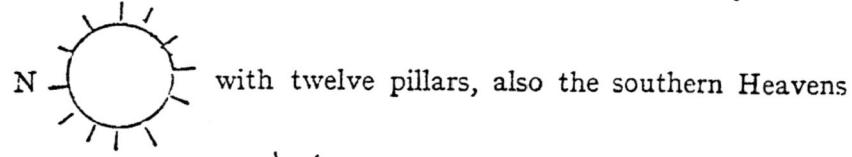

As regards some of the other signs and symbols that we use and which we find amongst, and in use as sacred symbols by, the Druids are the rough and smooth "A." The cube  was used by them first to signify truth and it was also a symbol of mercury. They represented the northern Heavens by a circle N with twelve pillars, also the southern Heavens as a circle S 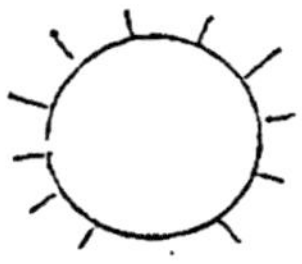 with twelve pillars, and these two circles were intersected in their centres by another smaller one with twelve pillars C  to represent the twelve signs of the Zodiac. The twelve in the north they called "Tywysogaethu"—"Leaders or Councillors," and the twelve in the south Heavens, "Cyfiawneon."

N. Heaven with twelve pillars. Small circle with twelve pillars to represent the twelve signs of the Zodiac.

S. Heaven with twelve pillars.

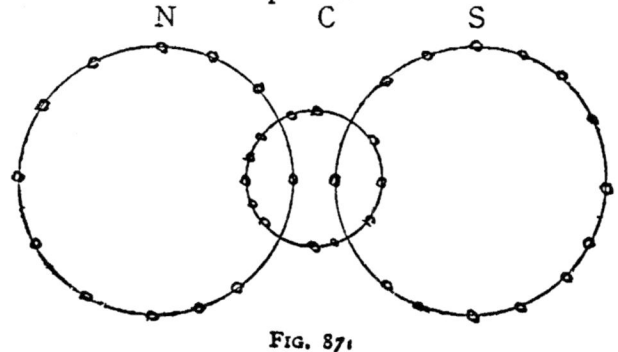

FIG. 871

PRIMORDIAL MAN

Heaven in thirty-six divisions also represented the thirty-six gates of "the Great House of him who is on the Hill"—*i.e.* the Great House of Heaven based upon the thirty-six gates or duodecams of the Zodiac.

When we were in Cornwall in 1904, inspecting some old Druidical remains, we came across a typical specimen, still existing, at Rough Tor, and took drawings of the same as here

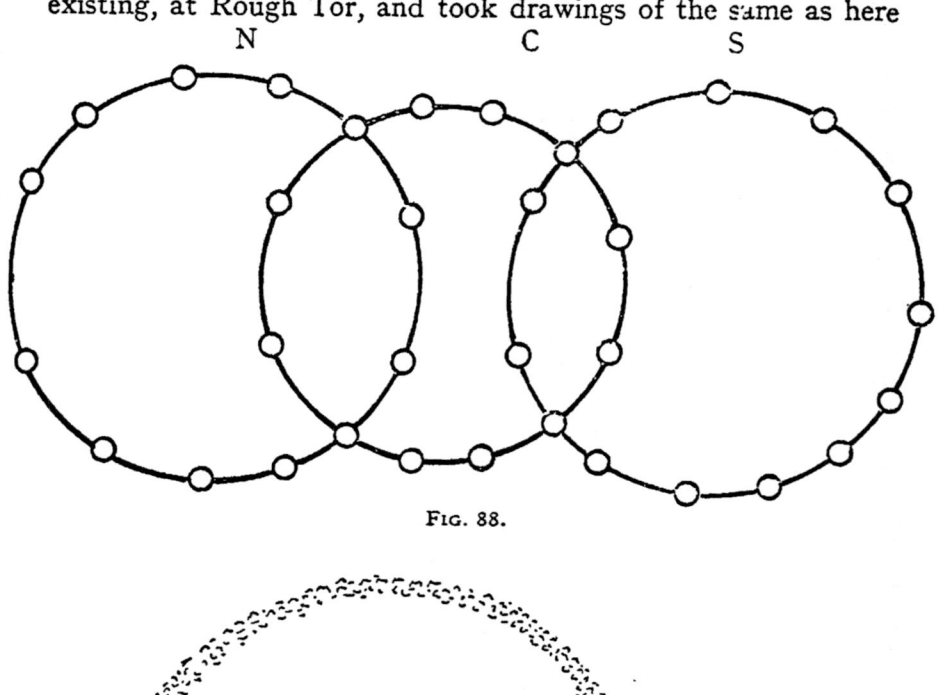

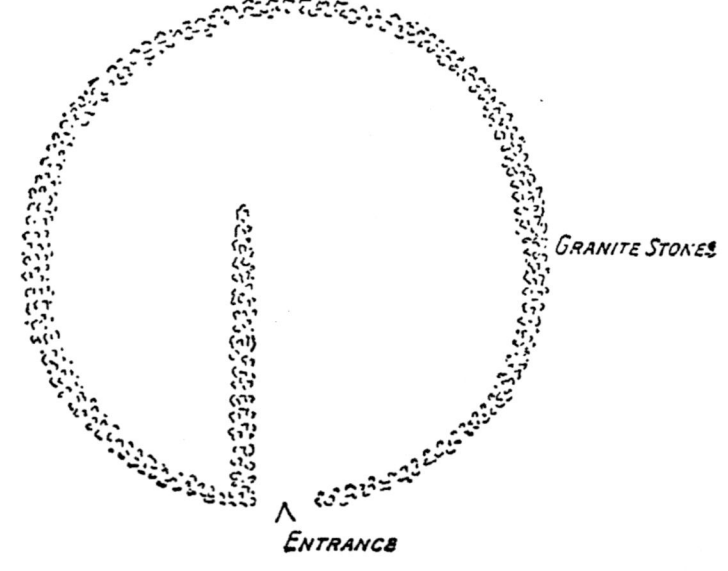

FIG. 88.

FIG. 89.

GRANITE STONES

ENTRANCE

depicted—two large circles, N. and S., and one smaller one intersecting these. Each had the so-called twelve pillars, and here they are called "Huts." A good specimen of one, almost perfect, still exists here; we give the drawing of this also, taken on the spot, and it shows the entrance E. by S. of all the smaller circles or Huts, so called, or "Pillars." All these we found at Rough Tor, in Cornwall. It appears to us that *Sir Norman Lockyer* (in his article in *Nature*, April 1906), in speaking of *two* circles at Tregeseal, has overlooked the lesser, which must have bisected the two greater circles. In all our researches in Cornwall we have been able to trace the remains of the *three* circles, and at Rough Tor these are very distinct. It is quite possible, however, to overlook the three here if you have not the "key," but to anyone who will mount Rough Tor some fifty or a hundred feet above the circles and then look down, the three can be seen quite distinctly. Then, if we count the "Stone Huts"[1] of each, and can understand the meaning and reasons for which these circles were erected, we shall know that they represented the three divisions of the heavens celestially, and the thirty-six nomes of Egypt terrestrially, which, of course, is a somewhat different view from that of *Sir Norman Lockyer*. Of course, his third circle may have been destroyed, as the farmers make hedges with these stones.

These three stone circles of the Druids must not be confounded or associated in any way with the "artificial mounds" we find throughout the world, all of which bear a striking resemblance. There is one at Salisbury Hill, at Avebury, 170 feet high, which is connected with ramparts—avenues 1480 yards long, circular ditches or "Dew Pans," and stone circles. Many of these are to be found in England, Ireland, and North and Central America, which are almost precisely similar. These are the remains of the "Towns" or dwellings of Neolithic man, situated on hills or downs, and ramparts were thrown up to keep off wolves and other wild animals from their cattle. The "avenues" were made for their cattle to pass through, morning and night, as they were driven to and from their pasture. The stone circles marked the places of the "huts" for the "keeper and look-out," and the

[1] We found that it was a good thing to "whitewash" these stones first. Of course it must not be forgotten that they also portrayed the Heavens—first in the seven divisions, then in eight, nine, ten and twelve—so we may find amongst the more ancient remains stones only of one of these divisions of the Heavens approximately giving the date of erection.

"dew pans," which were a peculiar construction, were made to contain their water supply. Early Neolithic man thus lived and protected his cattle from the ravages of wild animals, he having only stone axes, clubs, arrows, flint-heads and spears to use against many ferocious beasts, therefore many would dwell together on the top of the down or hill, throwing up ramparts of earth and digging ditches under them so that wolves and other animals could not easily get up to their flocks, which they drove in at night to keep secure. Here we see the first formation of "Towns" and "Cities" and man beginning to settle down in one place, instead of leading the nomadic life of their Paleolithic fathers. We draw attention to this as we have seen it stated that these "Mounds" have been attributed to the Druids by some writers. They are anterior to the Druids and are only to be associated with Neolithic man, and at the time of Stellar mythos; whereas the three circles were erected only by the Druids during Solar mythos, and are of much later date.

Diodorus Seculus gives the number of the nomes in Egypt as *thirty-six*. This symbol of the three circles of the Druids, therefore, would also represent the thirty-six nomes of Egypt at the time the Druids left Egypt *during the Solar Mythos*, and somewhat approximately fixes the date, as we know that the Egyptians were continually adding and increasing the number of nomes from the original seven up to forty-six. Historians have differed as to the number of nomes in Egypt and the reason is that with the Astral Mythology they mapped out seven in the heavens first of all and depicted the seven in the earth, and from them circles of twelve divisions, each of which, no doubt, was first astronomical, the three twelves had gradually increased from seven, ten, twelve to thirty-six. We know that not only did they map out the Northern division of the heavens but also the Southern and Central, therefore it is quite certain that here we find that they divided the North into twelve, the Central into twelve, and the South into twelve, making in all thirty-six; and, as they mapped out the heavens in a Celestial form, so they depicted the same in Terrestrial form.

That the Druids brought this with them from Egypt is also certain, because they could not map out the Southern heavens here—*these could not be seen here*, and it would only be possible to do this when near the Equator—here only could the Northern,

Southern and Central heavens be mapped out by the ancient astronomers, and this we know that the Egyptians did very thoroughly, and their Priests took this knowledge with them to whatever part of the world they went; hence the remains of these ancient monuments we find in various parts of the world and the true explanation of the same. We challenge anyone to gainsay and prove differently.

These three circles are not only found in the British Isles, but in various parts of the world, and these are proofs alone which suggest how many thousands of years before the Babylonians and Sumarians ever existed that the knowledge of the architecture of the heavens, North, Central and South was worked out and known to the old Priests of Egypt; and how any man, of such eminent knowledge as *Dr W. Budge*, should state " that the Egyptians borrowed their knowledge of the signs of the Zodiac, together with much else, *from the Greeks, etc.*,"[1] is beyond comprehension!! Even the Mayas had the knowledge before the Greek nation or Babylonians existed, and it is a question if the Druids were not much older than the Mayas. Numbers of these circles may be found in Devonshire and Cornwall, especially Cornwall, and because the Greeks, at the latter period of the Egyptian Dynasty, were employed to paint Dendera and perhaps some other temples, is no reason or proof to any thinking man, who has such contrary and conclusive facts still extant, that the Greeks introduced the signs of the Zodiac into Egypt, and we feel sure, from the great knowledge that *Dr Budge* possesses, that he really does not believe it to be a fact. Perhaps he is afraid, if he published the whole of his knowledge on these subjects, " that he might be placed in a similar position as *Dr Ray Lancaster* has been."

These must not be confounded with the two circles ○○ which were pre-Solar however, and twelve stones erected to form each—one to the north and one to the south representing the 24 zodiacal stars, and as characters in the Egyptian learning these earliest pre-Solar powers constituted " the old ones " or " the Elders." These are Egyptian wherever found and are traceable to two different groups of 12=the 24 mysteries of the Stellar Mythos. These were the 12 who had their thrones as rulers

---

[1] " The Gods of Egypt," vol. ii. page 312.

PRIMORDIAL MAN

(or æons) in the Zodiac and the 12 as spirits with Horus-Khuti, Lord of the Spirits in the heaven of eternity. In the papyrus of Ani and of Nunefer we see the Judges in the Maat appear as 12 in number sitting on 12 thrones and we find these two circles in Cornwall distinguishable from the three.

"Where did our ancient brethren meet before lodges were erected? upon 'holy ground'; on the highest hill or lowest vale or any other secret place, the better to guard against cowans and enemies"; and we have distinct records left that when St Augustine came to these Isles in the sixth century to convert the "*Heathern Natives*" to Christianity, he found numerous priests and their disciples here, and who had *been* here "for all time that was known," who were distinguished for the pure religion which they practised and professed. These were the so-called "Culdees," and many joined the "Christian Church" and became priests of the same, and were merged into it after the close of the twelfth century, although many kept themselves aloof for a long period after. These were the last remnants of the old Druid Priests—descendants of their Egyptian brethren—who practised the pure Eschatology of their forefathers. Gradually they all died out as a separate and distinct class, and those who remained were merged into "Christianity," but they brought on all the doctrines with them and practised these in secret places, in so-called lodges, and these exist to the present day as "Freemasons." The ceremonies have been somewhat changed, and innovations have been made to suit the evolution of the times, but still Freemasonry is the purest of all the relics of our forefathers, and in Egypt alone do we find the origin. (*See* Appendix 3.)

No regular history of the order at this time can be found, nor is it necessary to our purpose. We know that their open worship was prohibited by this edict of Canute here in England, who reigned from 1015 to 1036. Some time, therefore, during this period, the edict was issued, and they were forbidden to perform their devotions. To evade the minions of the law, they resorted to private meetings and secret celebrations, and we do not entertain any doubt that these formed the first so-called "Lodges" in England, as a cloak to screen their religious rites and ceremonies and to keep them pure as they had received them originally from the parent sources in Egypt. It is impossible to state if this took the form of "Craft Masonry" first in England or Scotland. The Druids were first persecuted and driven to secret meetings in England, as may be seen from the above edict, but all that is immaterial to us, and we only mention it because the Scotch people claim to be the "oldest masons." Our contention is that the Druids were the direct descendants of the High Priests of Egypt, who came over here. Their beliefs, forms, rites and ceremonies were the same, and our brotherhood—Freemasonry—has been carried on ever since, and is one and the same thing.

The allied Degrees—Degrees are quite arbitrary—contain much innovation in some of the parts, and many of these have been interpolated by members who have travelled and been initiated in the so-called "Eleusinian Mysteries," which were those founded in various centres of the world by men who had been to Egypt and had learned some of the doctrines of the Priests there. When they returned to their own country they founded so-called "Schools" and sects of the order. Hence, to gain the correct knowledge of the whole of our degrees, it is necessary to know these and the Egyptian *Ritual*, and the knowledge of their progressive evolution for the development of their mythos to Astronomical Mythology, Stellar, Lunar and Solar; and finally their Eschatology, to appreciate the knowledge of all our signs and symbols, etc., taking into consideration at the same time what evolution and time have brought about.

What is that which is lost? And where do you expect to find it? The reason that we go from East to West in search of that which is lost is because, when Osiris lost his life by the machinations of Sut, like all the Manes he travelled from East to West to enter Amenta. There, in Amenta, after passing through difficulties, dangers and darkness, his Manes was regenerated or raised again in the form of Amsu, or Horus, in spirit, and he came forth from Amenta after entering the West, to the glorious gate of the East again, as a raised Manes or glorified spirit in the form of Ra ☉.

He *returned to the East with all the secrets of Amenta.* Here it was, in Amenta, that the Tatt Cross was thrown down; here it was that the Veil of the Temple was rent asunder and the C. S. poured forth blood and water, and all was reborn; here he was shown all the signs and given or taught those passwords, or words of power and might that kept evil and the powers of darkness away, and enabled him to advance from one Aāt to the next.

The Tatt Pillar was re-erected and the dead Osiris was reborn as the Child Horus, and came forth as the glorified spirit Ra ☉; or the dead man had here been raised to this glorious resurrection in spirit form. The final password and sign had been given him, the highest degree conferred, and to him who was in possession of [hieroglyphs] all doors were open, both in this life and the life hereafter.[1]

Ta-Ua to Am-Ur is the Egyptian for E. to W.

Here we have the answer which solves the question of "who and what were our ancient Druids?" They were undoubtedly descendants of the ancient Egyptian priests, who came over and landed in Ireland and the West of England, and who brought with them their religious doctrines and taught and practised them here. The Tuatha-de-Dananns, who came to Ireland, were of the same race and spoke the same language as the Fir-Bolgs and the Formarians, possessed ships, knew the art of navigation, had a compass or magnetic needle, worked in metals, had a large army, thoroughly organised, and a body of surgeons; had a "Bardic or Druid class of priests." These "Druids" brought all their learning with them, believed and practised the Eschatology of the Solar doctrines, and all came from Egypt. That their temples are older than those found in Uxmal, in Yucatan, in Mexico (which are stated to be 11,500 years old) and those amongst the Incas in South America, and some of the Zimbabwe in South Africa, is clearly proved by their want of knowledge in building an arch, although we find in the oldest remains amongst the Zimbabwe lintels at Umnukwana, and no doubt there are others in South African ruins, but successive immigrants have obliterated most of the original, which was the old Egyptian, as can be proved by other facts.

The Incas had the same wonderful and skilful way of building as the Egyptians—that is, they so prepared and finished huge blocks of stone, and fitted them so accurately, that it is almost impossible to distinguish where the joints are. This was done by a very fine cement, made with granite, which blended with the blocks, and made it perfect. This we also find amongst the ruins

---

[1] The word, sign and T. of the 30° was taken from Anhuri. An interesting plate of this in Egyptian is shown in Maspero's work, "Dawn of Civilisation," p. 99.
Satit presenting Pharaoh Amenôthes III. to Khnûmû, from the Temple of Khnûmû at Elephantine, shows precisely the S—— of ——.

at Umnukwana and all the *ancient* part of the ruins called the Great Zimbabwe.

But the ancient Egyptians did not build arches until a later date. The first true arch is found in a Fourth Dynasty Mastaba, at Medum—one always finds lintels. This is the case with the Druidical temples; but at Uxmal we find that the arch has taken the place of the lintel. We have no doubt either, from the character of the hieroglyphics and their significance, that this temple or tomb of Ollamh Fodhla was built at the time of the Lunar or early Solar mythos. The arches we find in Central America are built in the same way and form as we find the Egyptians and early Greeks built them—that is, *one stone overlapping the other*. This may be proved by comparing those of Las Monjas, Palenque, with the Egyptian Fourth and Fifth Dynasty arches, and " The Treasure-House " at Athens.

In " Neu Manners and the Auld of Scottis," *Boea* says the old inhabitants used the rights and manners of the Egyptians, from whom they took their beginning. In all their secret business they wrote with cyphers and figures of beasts, made in the manner of letters.

The ancient Britons buried the beetle with their dead, the same as the Egyptians, and the same genus—the *Dermestes*. It was the emblem of time, ever renewing—a symbol of eternity. The scarab not only represented the circle of the sun, but the renewing cycles of the soul.

The Hebrew Gev is identical with the Egyptian Khef and the children of Khef. The Æthiopic Genetrix are designated the Gentiles, who went northward out of Egypt and carried with them the primordial name of the birthplace in the Celestial North —the race of Japheth is the same as the race of Kheft, and we learn from CANUTE'S EDICT that the Druids were called Gentiles here at that time.

How many years the Druids lived and practised their ceremonies and religious rites in Britain is not known, but when Christianity was introduced into these isles there would be, no doubt, a " war waged " against " the heathen," and as the former spread and increased, so the other would naturally die out as Druids, but the few who remained would still carry on their mysteries secretly, and as many of their signs, symbols and rituals were the same as taught by Moses, naturally they would become absorbed into the later doctrines.

PRIMORDIAL MAN

According to *Cæsar*, the Druids taught the Gauls that they were all descended from Dis Pater, the Demiurge—that is, from the god of Hades, or Amenta, who is Tanan, as consort of the goddess Tanen, and whose name was taken by Ptah-Tanan, the better known Dis Pater who was earlier than Osiris, in the Egyptian Mythology, and from whom the Solar race *ascended*, whether from Puanta, or the Tuat.

To understand this, it is necessary to know that Egypt represented the Tuat, and Amenta geographically. Lower Egypt was the representation of the Tuat, and Upper Egypt, of Amenta.

Thus interpreted, the Tuatha, or tribes who brought the *Ancient Solar wisdom out of Lower Egypt, or the " Tuat of Egypt," were genuine Egyptians*, and must not be confounded with the *manes* in Lower Egypt, in the book of Hades, which was not a geographical, but a mythical locality, in the earth of Eternity: the lower domain of the double earth, the country of the manes.

The wise men of Old Egypt understood that this was made by Ptah, and their religion at this period was the commencement of the Solar, and the exodus at this time bore the names here as it did in Egypt—*i.e.* what they portrayed celestially, and in the earth of Eternity, in their religious doctrines, they mapped out geographically.

Cæsar tells us also that Manannan, son of Lir, was patron of roads and journeys, and he was worshipped by the Gauls above all other gods. This is the Egyptian Ap-Uat, a form of Anup—the guide through Amenta, and was a god of the Pole Star, and lord of the Polar Paradise, before he fell from heaven, thus showing that previous to the Solar, they had the Stellar mythos. Another name for him was El Shaddai.

There are two points always to be considered in the departure of the human migrations from Egypt: one is from the summit of the Celestial Mounts—the other from the hollow underworld, beneath the Mount, or inside the earth, as these from the Tuat.

The races who *descended* from the Mount were people of the Pole, whose starting point and reckoning time were from one or other stations of the Pole Star, determinable by its Zootypes—these were Stellar.

Those who *ascended from* the nether world were Solar. Taking this point in conjunction with the others we have brought forward, we can trace approximately the time of the exodus from Egypt of the different tribes from all over the world, by tracing their Zootypes to the Constellation of the Pole Star, corresponding to it, but prior to the time that the Pole Star passed into the Constellation of Herakles, or the Man—or at the time of the Great Deluge of Manhu—*i.e.* when Herakles was replaced by another Pole Star.

Previous to this, the races were imaged by pre-human types, and the Great Mother was the origin of all; all was Stellar mythos, or Stellar-Lunar; after the Constellation of Herakles arrived, the Man superseded the Woman; Solar doctrines took the place of Stellar and Lunar, and the Fatherhood replaced the Motherhood.

The time of the exodus of the North American Indians and Samoans must have been at the time of the change of the Pole Star from Cygnus to Vega, in the Constellation of Lyra, about 18,000 or 20,000 years ago, according to their traditions and the Zootypes of their tribes or about 26,000 years before that.

All such origins as found in their Marchens are of course mythical and not historical or geographical, although the mythical land gets localised on the surface of the earth, geographically.

In explaining the story of the Deluge from tales found (from all over the world), there was not one, but seven—one at the change of each Pole Star, the hitherto reigning star sank down into the waters of space, and gave precedence to the next one in the cycle of precession, and therefore there was a deluge at the change of each Pole Star, 6—and the Great Deluge of all. The One=6+1=7, was when Herakles, the Man, sank down and was drowned in the Celestial water of space, the end of the Great Year, when all the Zootypes — the Tortoises, Apes, Bears, Serpents, etc. — were transformed into human beings—*i.e.* the creation of man, and the cycle of precession recommenced again. And the seven primary powers which had hitherto been portrayed by Zootypes, were now imaged in the earliest human form of man—as Ptah and his pygmies.

Here, then, we have the original ● dot, or "point within the centre of the circle, from which the M.M. cannot err" if he believes and so acts, etc.

First the dot ● or point is in the centre of a star with seven Rays or its summit. It signifies "The Supreme One,"

PRIMORDIAL MAN

and the seven glorious ones—The Master and the seven wise men. The seven Powers sustaining The One :—Horus, in Heaven situated at the Pole Star, with the seven glorious ones circulating round—*i.e.* the Stars composing the Little Bear. Heaven was, at this period, divided into two divisions, North and South— Light and Darkness, with Horus representing the North and Light, and Sut, the South, Night and Darkness sometimes represented by two circles with ⊙ above, with emblems of regal power—One name of Amsu, the risen Horus.

FIG. 90.

FROM MEXICAN CODICES

With the Ancient Egyptians, the highest land or summit of the Earth was at the Equator, called Ap-ta, and was then rendered mythically as the highest point of the Northern heavens —as the Apta in their Astronomical representations.

The Sources of the Nile—Equatorial provinces—where the great Lakes and the Papyrus swamps were, was their Ta-Nuter, or Holy Land—*i.e.* " The Land of the Spirits or gods," and the chief features of this earthly Paradise were repeated in the circum-polar high land.

The Sky, as the great Celestial water, was also divided into two great Lakes, one to the North and one to the South of the Mount of Bekhu on which heaven rested; these are mentioned in the *Ritual* as the Lake of Kharu, and the Lake of Ru— chaps. cviii.-cix. No doubt this was founded on the two great Lakes in Central Africa.

In Equatoria the two Pole Stars are seen resting on the horizon; the only two fixed stars in the firmament, and these were seen there, resting on the Poles or summit of the Mount, never setting—the two eyes or Merti, and were represented sometimes by two Jackals in the Kamite Astronomical Mythology— but first as the two Pillars, North and South.

As man travelled North, the Star and Pillar of Sut (South) sank down into the dark abyss, or the Nether World, and so Sut became the Power of Darkness in the Nether World—or Amenta. Travelling North, they would see the Stars of the two Bears, circling around the Pole Star, fixed on the Summit of the Mount of the North—the farther North they came, the farther these would be lifted up, and it is here that Shu lifts up the Heavens (Mythically). The Pole Star for ever rested on the horizon at the Equatoria, and so Shu lifted up the heavens, as the nomads travelled North.

There were no Solstices in Apta, it was equal day and equal night, so that when Shu upraised the sky, it was equally divided into two parts, between Horus and Sut. The rising and setting of the stars were vertical, and the two fixed centres of the Poles, were on the two horizons; or, as the Egyptians explained it, on the North and South of the Mount of the Earth.

The Pole Star was a type of the Eternal because, apparently, it never changed with time; it was the earliest type of supreme intelligence which gave the law in heaven which was unerring, just and true, and it became a standpoint in the heavens for the mind of man to rest on at the centre, and radiate to the circumference, "a point within a circle from which you could not err."

The Eye on the Mount, or the point ● within the centre of the circle, was a type of Anup, and the earliest law in heaven was given on the Mount because the Mount was an image of the Pole, and Anup administered the law as the Judge—the Jackal in Egypt was a Zootype for the Judge.

Gerald Massey has attributed Anup (Jackal) on the Mount to a form of Sut at the North, but we differ from him, and for this reason. On the planisphere of Denderal the two Poles are represented by two Jackals, or two Eyes, the North that of Horus and the South that of Sut; therefore we attribute the Anup of the North to a type of Horus and not Sut, who was the first god of the Pole Star which was South (the Southern Heavens were mapped out first, as proved by the *Ritual*) and as the Southern Pole Star sank down into darkness and was lost to view as they migrated north, so the Northern Pole Star would rise and supersede it in the Pole Star of Horus—Anup, and it was only the Northern migration, people who at this time advanced in stature and wisdom, and spread over the world. There is sufficient evidence in the *Ritual* to prove this as well as tracing the people of the various exodes. A type in the Egyptian may be variously applied, and may not always determine the nature of the deity, but the Jackal denotes the Judge, and the Judge in heaven here, in the North, was Horus: of course it was not the Mount which was the divinity, or the Jackal, but the power which dwelt upon it, as portrayed by the type.

The power of stability, fixed as the centre of the Universe, was the typical Eternal, and the Stars—*i.e.* Ursa Minor (The Stars which never set — Rit) constituted the circumpolar O, the starry types of eternal powers.

In all Mythologies, the Pole Star is an emblem of stability, a seat, or throne of the Power which is the highest god—Anup or Horus in Egypt, Sydik in Phœnicia, Anu in Babylonia, Tai-Yih in China, Avather or Zivo in Mesopotamia, Ame-No-Foko-Tachi-Kami in Japan and various other names for the same in different parts of the world.

In Rig-Veda the habitation of the one god is placed in the highest North, "beyond the seven Rishes"; these are by some supposed to be represented by the Stars of the GREAT BEAR, but it is not so; these seven Rishes—Urshi, or Divine Watchers—were grouped in URSA MINOR, "the Stars of which constellation never set." These were the chief of the Akhemu under Anup, the god of the Pole Star, the Subbas, or Mandozs, "the Ancients of the Mesopotamia," who are still followers of the old Egyptian Stellar Mythos.

In the next progressive evolution, we have the Sacred Triangle as the Emblem of Heaven in three divisions, with Shu added at the Equinox to the North and South, thus forming the original Trinity. The above was all formed and worked out by the old wise men during the Stellar Mythos.

FIG. 91.[1]

Progressing further, we find that they had now mapped out Heaven or "Built the Heavens on the Square" with the four children of Horus at the four corners, as the supports thereof, and finally Ptah completed the tunnelling through the Earth and formed Amenta as a passage for Ra the Sun, Taht the Moon and the Manes. In the complete Put-Cycle of Ptah, we have the Heavens in a circle in nine divisions, then in ten divisions, and finally in twelve; and then twelve signs of the Zodiac were com-

[1] Triangle associated with Horus only.

204 SIGNS AND SYMBOLS OF

pleted and filled in. The Heaven in eight divisions was formed when Taht was added to the seven Stellar, and was therefore Lunar.

As the Sun, or Ra, rose in the East to diffuse Light and Glory to men on this Earth, so when it "set in the West" it entered Amenta—"the land of the Nether World" to diffuse its light and glory to "the Manes there"; it made its passage from West to East, rising again at the East here, ever completing its circle as time rolled on.

This was Solar Mythos, and the Eschatology which follows is explained, separately, in other parts of this work.

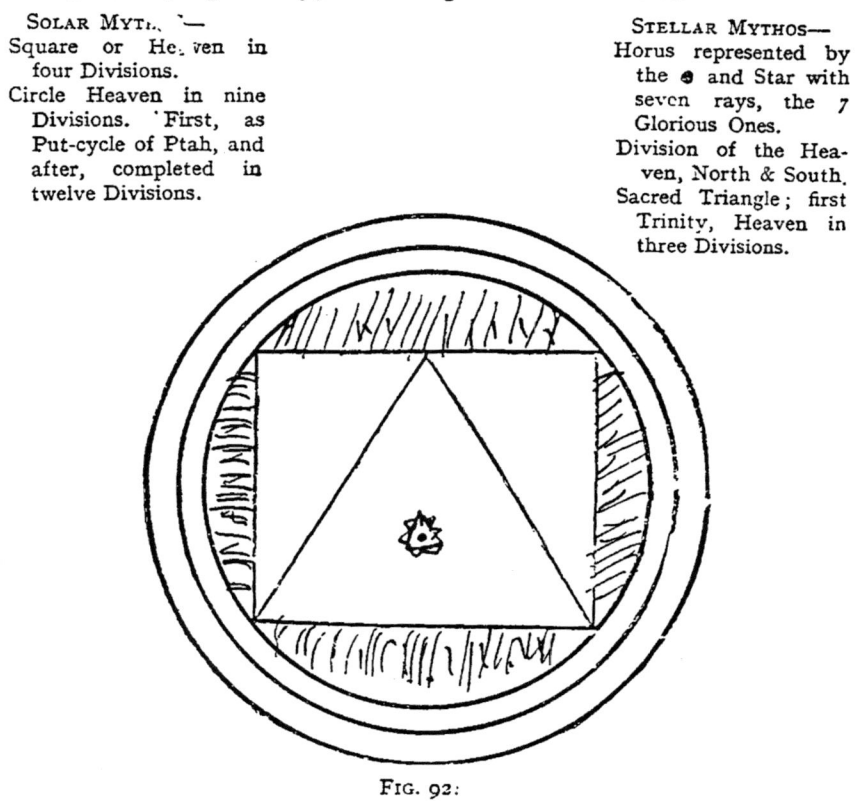

SOLAR MYTHOS.—
Square or Heaven in four Divisions.
Circle Heaven in nine Divisions. First, as Put-cycle of Ptah, and after, completed in twelve Divisions.

STELLAR MYTHOS—
Horus represented by the ☉ and Star with seven rays, the 7 Glorious Ones.
Division of the Heaven, North & South.
Sacred Triangle; first Trinity, Heaven in three Divisions.

FIG. 92.

The mysteries of Osiris, Isis and Horus, though the latest in evolution, have been given the foremost place in the *Ritual*, and have somewhat obscured the pre-Osirian Mythology, but Atum was the Great Judge upon the Mount of Amenta at a far earlier period than Osiris.

THE GOD AMSU.
The rising spirit of mummied Horus in the Mythos, and of Osiris in the Eschatology
He holds the whip of power— the Egyptian Khu—in one hand pointing above, H.A
The other is not free yet from the swathing bandages, and is pointing downwards, H.D.
The Good Shepherd

The Cable-Tow

How many of our fraternity know the true import and meaning of the " Cable-tow " ? Originally it was a chain or rope, of some kind, worn by the I. or those about to be initiated, to signify their belief in God and their dependence on Him, and their solemn obligations to submit and devote themselves to His will and service, and the fact that he is neither naked nor clothed is an emblem that he is untutored—a mere child of nature—unregenerate and destitute of any knowledge of the true God, as well as being destitute of the comforts of life. This is the state in which we find all candidates. The chain was used by the Druids and Egyptians as a symbolism, as stated above. Also that he was being led from darkness into light, from ignorance to knowledge of the one true and living God, Creator and Judge of all things in heaven and earth. Here we have the origin of the Cable-tow in the Eschatology.

Father Burgo's description of the Zapotecs, Mexicans and Mayas, and also *Juan de Cordova*, speaking of " Tola, a grass-like plant, (una yerva de los ervazales), out of which they made a straw rope, (una sozuilla o' tonuza), which they brought to confession and laid down on the ground before the pijana and confessed what sin they wished to confess, etc," gives you a very wrong impression, and their translation is not correct, because " Tola " here they make the meaning of as " sin " and " lao-Tola " place of sin or confession, but this is wrong ; the meaning of the word is " a dark place," and the ceremonies observed and described by the above show how ignorant they were of the true meaning of the ceremony, which was the same as that of the first degree in Freemasonry, and the " rope of straw was not to hang the young man with," as all I.'s well know—although in some Glyphs the rope appears around the neck.

That the rope appears around the neck of more than one, in these picture scenes (seven in some) is only a symbol of the seven powers—as " the seven ropes," and each one of the wearers of these represents one of the seven powers or attributes of Horus I. in their sacerdotal duties. Originally it was one only which was associated with Horus I. and Amsu (the risen Horus or Horus in the Spirit). This is well depicted in the accompanying photograph of Amsu. The Cable-tow is seen hanging down his back; it has been removed from the neck (earthly type). Horus, having been led or passed through dangers, difficulties, darkness and death in the underworld, emerges as Amsu, the first risen man-God, and attached to his crown of two feathers (denoting the two lives, earthly and Spiritual) is this Cable-tow or rope—as a symbol that it is " a power " which has led him through from earthly to Spiritual life.

In the same way was the boat of Osiris dragged through the underworld by a rope, by the " powers " we find mentioned in the *Ritual* as he was dragged in, led through darkness into light, came forth in the double cave, and emerged as Ra in a Spiritual form—one and the same—the former being the Stellar and oldest, and the latter the Solar or Osirian: in our case we apply it symbolically in the Christian.

The origin of the " Blazing Star " was the Egyptian " Sothos," and shown as Anubis, who guided the soul through Amenta, and its allusion as the star which guided the " wise men," etc., is a recent version of the old, and one which does not require further explanation (see *Ritual*), and which is found many times in the Mexican and Maya pictures and glyphs. (*See* Appendix 4.)

" The Bright Morning Star," the Star with eight rays, also represents Horus of the resurrection or Jesus. It originally represented " Orion," the eightfold one—the highest. The seven, with the essence of these added to make " THE ONE "—*i.e.* eight.

In Revelation the Son of God promises to give the Morning Star to him that overcometh, " as I also have received of my Father: I will give him the Morning Star," Rev. ii. 28. The Morning Star was equally identified with Horus, " I know the power of the East, Horus of the Solar Mount, the Calf in presence of the God and the Star of Dawn," *Ritual*, chap. cix.; henceforth the Morning Star was given to the followers of Horus, therefore we use it.

It was the Star of Horus and his guide which led him to Paradise when he seated himself upon his Throne, and then Horus gave his Star as a guide to his followers (see *Ritual*).

Perhaps nothing shows or demonstrates so well the universal evolution and the origin of all our Signs, Symbols and PW's, and how they have been brought on from the primordial and the

CHAPTER IX

DRUIDS AND ISRAELITES

The religion of the Druids was similar in all particulars to that of the Israelites and Mayas. If we compare the recorded practices of the ancient Israelites with the remaining relics of Druidical customs, both internal and foreign evidences prove their similarity. They both believed in one God, the Creator, Preserver and Ruler of all things, the life and soul of the world, who endures for ever and exists throughout space.

The names given to the Supreme Being by the Druids and Hebrews point out in a still more definite manner the identity of the two Deities. The Israelites were accustomed to adore God under the title of Bel or Baal—the original name for Jehovah—" Thou shalt call me Ishi and shalt call me no more Baali "—Hosea ii. 16. With the Druids Bel was the Supreme God. The sacred name of the Lord להוה had also its equivalent term amongst the British Druids: Hu was an epithet of Bel, signifying the self-existent Being:—" He that is." The similarity in sound of the two names and the near relation between " He that is " and " I am that I am " must be evident to the most superficial student (see further chapter on Cross).

The great similarity existing between the Druidical, Maya and Israelitish rites will appear from the following:—

Grove worship was equally prevalent amongst the Israelites as amongst the Druids: it was in the recesses of groves that the Druids exercised some of the mystic rites and taught their votaries the worship of the true God. Abraham planted a grove in Beersheba and called then on the name of the Lord: and after, when the family of Abraham had greatly increased, journeying Northward after leaving their native country, they were strictly commanded to cut down the groves of the people whom they destroyed:—" Ye shall destroy their altars, break their statues and cut down their groves " (Exod. xxxiv. 13), ancient Egyptian Stellar, Lunar and Solar Mythos, added to when necessary, or altered in name to suit the Priests of various ages, as the SSW of the so-called 90° of the Mysteries of Mizram (Hebrew for Egypt). These mysteries are the same as the Mysteries of Memphis, all of which we know and are perfectly acquainted with. They are somewhat similar to our Freemasonry in all its degrees; but we have compressed their 90° into 33°. The Egyptian PW and A are "I and O" in the highest degree, but the English Freemasons do not recognise any connection with these. We are of opinion that our Freemasonry is purer and a truer copy of the *Ritual* than the others, which contain innovations.

The original Pole Star with dot ✹ represented Horus I. This, with Triangle, was Stellar. The square was Solar, first portrayed at the time of Ptah when he completed Amenta and built the heavens on the square by adding E. and W. to N. and S. with four supports—the four children of Horus.